The Unraveling

Briare Jones

BookLeaf
Publishing

Presentation by *BookLeaf Publishing*

Web: www.bookleafpub.com

E-mail: info@bookleafpub.com

ISBN: 9789358312454

First edition 2023

Twerking in Confidence

Growing up shaking your ass
Was deemed inappropriate
By the adults
Exciting for the boys
empowering for the girls
For me it was scary
And still is scary
What if I don't shake the right way?
What if there's not enough jiggle?
What if it's not exciting enough?
There it is
The fear of judgment and not being enough
Moving my body in such a sensual way when I
am alone
Is so empowering
I feel connected to my sensual side and I want to
share the energy
And experience with my partner
Only when the opportunity arises I freeze
What if I'm not enough?
So one afternoon I played along
And I shook some ass ashamed and scared
He told me I was sexy and need to be more
confident.

Earlier that day he corrected my posture by
pushing my shoulders back
He told me i need to be confident
I hadn't realized that I was still shrinking
That some part of me still feels the need to hide
And find solace and comfort within
That I still feel small
Since then I try to be more confident in myself
To not let my shoulders shrink
I try to not shrink within myself and hide away
I try to not be ashamed of myself
For simply just being
Or for shaking some ass
Because it feels good
To be woman
It feels good to shake what your mama gave ya
It feels good to be me
unapologetically
It's also frightening

Strapless

I don't like wearing bra's
I only wear them when I need to keep
everything in place
Bra's feel constricting
And suffocating
When I'm at home I wear no bra
Sometimes my nipples show through my shirt
So I cower and hide my chest
Or I use my arms to cover my nipples
Why do I feel the need to hide my body?
She is beautiful
She is art.
Why am I concerned that my nipples
Poking through my shirt
Will cause me danger ?
Why am I ashamed?
Everyone has nipples
There is no need to be ashamed.
Maybe it's because my shoulders tempt men to
sin
And my legs cause them to fall right in
Maybe because my body has been a playground
For others to explore
And my breast have felt unwarranted wandering
hands

When trying to rest
Or maybe because media says a woman's
nipples are explicit
But what about men's?
Oh we're allowed to stare at their pecks
Watch them undress
While they try to impress
Everyone has nipples
Let them be free

The Silencing

It started in grade school
Where I learned amongst many things
That using my voice
Simply speaking
Could get me in trouble
My stick constantly moved from green to red
Based upon how much I talked in class
I get it
There's a time and place for everything
including speaking
So I learned that being a "chatterbox" isn't the
best thing to be
I learned to be quiet or as quiet as I can be

Then it started in conversation
Constantly being cut off and dismissed
Like I wasn't saying anything at all

Then in discipline
most things I keep to myself

Wouldn't want to upset anyone or get popped in
the mouth
I learned that verbally expressing myself was a
problem,
disrespectful, and shouldn't be done.

Even now in the workplace
God forbid your employees actually like each
other and converse
Are we meant to be robots ?
Learn and do as we're told ?
Are we not allowed to have fun?
or converse and connect?
Why do you take my voice as a threat?
Even if i'm silenced
I still have paper and pen

Change

Looking back
Change has always been hard for me
I remember the last day of kindergarten
I cried
I loved my teacher and I enjoyed all the things
we did in class
I thought i was never going to see Ms. C again
I did though in the halls on my way to 1st grade

At some point during my journey down the hall
It started to feel like everyone was talking about
me
Not in a good way
I felt singled out
Like I stood out as if something were wrong
with me

I guess I've always known that I am different

I was never really one to have friends.
I was in my own world
I didn't really engage with the other kids and I
kept to myself

In third grade I started to notice the other kids
and the way they engaged with each other
I started to understand the concept of friendship
I carried a journal and I wrote in it
They often made fun of me for it
They didn't like me
At least not enough to be friends with me

Third grade my parents got divorced
I started pulling my hair out
I remember pulling it out sitting in the back
during math class
The other kids called me a crackhead when I
was stressing

Fourth grade I tried to make friends and was
bullied in return
My teachers didn't care
In fact they punished me for asking for help

Since then I haven't really had the best of luck
making friends
People come and go
I understood that as not being enough
When that's not what it was

Dear Little B,

I'm so sorry
For everything
You know if there was anything
 I could change
Or do different
It would be the way I showed up for you
I wouldn't let people walk all over us
Like a doormat
Smearing their dirt and mud
On our heart
I wouldn't let their hurt and pain
Become our own
Everything isn't for us to carry
I would tell you
It's okay to put down the weight
Or share it
To be confident
Pursue the things you love
I would remind you of your worth,
How beautiful you are,
And better guard your heart
But we are here now
and I am no time traveler
I can and will do those things now
Little B
"I'm ready to be there for you
Like you've always been for me" ~ Hailey Knox

Come out and Play

well , well, well
Look what we have here

Look who's finally ready to come out of their
shell
The world can be a scary place
I know
Darling, we've been waiting for you
It's time to shine

Puddles

What would happen…
If I bursted into to tears
Showed you all my fear
Or is that too real?

Will you catch me when I fall?
Or watch me drown
Screaming for help

Understanding

Growing up I came to understand
Comfort was bad
That it is better to be uncomfortable
In some weird way being uncomfortable was the
goal
It resembled growth and progress
If you were comfortable then you were as stale
As the open bag of chips no one's touched in the
cabinet

I came to understand that I was not enough on
my own
I needed some god to come and make me whole
Then and only then would I be good and never
alone
Yet I felt so lonely even in a room full with
abstract souls

I came to understand that I was the problem
Only I wasn't

There is nothing wrong with me.
There is nothing wrong with being comfortable
In fact we are creatures of comfort
and i'm tired of the discomfort in my body

Tensing in my shoulder blades
Aching in my lower back
Tightening in my neck
and the heaviness in my chest
Pulling my shoulders to the ground

I think we should challenge ourselves within
reason
Dance through fear when it arises
live life fiercely
Freely

Meltdowns

Sometimes I get this feeling
When others are upset with me
That I'm an embarrassment
This voice gushes nothing but punishment
For the crimes that we do
"Why were you talking? You're
So annoying. Everyone was right
You do too much"
and it hurts
Like a sad dog in the rain
So I walk away
That's what my dad did and he wasn't the only
one
when they said such things
So I figured it's best I go away
The world is dark and cold
When you go alone
My vibe fly too high
Hard to resonate
I change the room
add an element
When I'm gone
They be missing it
There's nothing like the sting of being dismissed
Or ignored

What's it matter
No one cares
Why is it I'm too much
And if I'm too much
Then how could I be not enough
Call it dramatic

SHHHHHHHH!!!!!!!

Oh right ….
I'm rambling

NO. 21

I've been feeling weighed down
All the heaviness in my shoulders
I've been feeling sad and anxious
and this overwhelming urge to cry
I can swallow it for now
But it won't be long til it resurfaces
It just won't stay down.
Why am I crying ?
I have nothing to cry about
My phone's been dying
I'm working two jobs
Nothing feels right
I invalidate myself
Because that's what they taught me
Instead of self regulation

I snapped at my coworker this morning
For her lack of communication
Then apologized shortly after
I didn't like my tone
Plus i wasn't really mad at her
No
I'm just in the valley,
In the dark

Rattled and frantically searching for the light
switch
Jamming my fingers
Stubbnig my toes
I can't seem to feel it out
What exactly has me spiraling
Why can't I sleep at night
Why I feel this overwhelming urge to cry
Why am I so moody and sensitive
I can't find what's wrong with me
To fix it
Will you leave me?
I'm scared to be abandoned

I'm only being human
Imperfect
After all I am not a robot

Behavior is communication
The lights on the dashboard
Telling you something needs a little more tlc
Time, love, and attention

I need to slow down
Take a look at my plate
Reevaluate
Be gentle and kind
Show myself grace and patience
I need self compassion

It's okay to cry
Even if it's about nothing
Crying is a form of release
My body is just communicating my needs
I need a little more help right now and that's
okay
Everyone is their own type of unique
Every plant has its own care plan
Made to fit their needs
Some need more light than others
Some thrive in the desert
My point is
It's okay if my needs do not look the same as
everyone else's.
It's okay if their needs are different from mine .

"What's Wrong?"

Ask me, "What's wrong?"
So I can tell you I don't know…
Everything and nothing at all

What do you do when everything feels out of
control?
When there's an empty void filling with a
sadness
Nobody knows ?
My parents didn't know
Or they didn't know how to cope
My mom just tells me to pray it away
My dad tells me to keep my head up
That i have to be strong
I've had to be strong since i was young
I am tired
I want to fall apart

Bad Weather

I hate when the weather gets bad
Everyone leaves
No one wants to play
Then it's just me
Holding big emotions that scare me
and everyone else too
Its draining for you
Its draining for me
I'll understand if you leave
Cause that's what people do
…
leave

My Depression

My depression make me feel unlovable
Especially when it's Severe
I'm easily irritated
Short tempered
Extremely emotional
And sensitive
It can be draining
It leaves me exhausted
The sadness comes in waves
It washes over me and I'm tossed in the currents
Trying to find space to breathe only I'm
drowning.
It feels like everyone leaves
When the weather gets bad In my head
Whether it's cause they have too much on their
plate
Or they don't know how to help
What to do
I'm no fun to be around during a severe episode
I delete all my social medias
I have thoughts like no one would miss me
I try to do it all on my own
I get frustrated
I don't know how to help myself
I'm using my tools trying to stay grounded

And it seems nothing is working
If you see me crying
Try not too worry too much
I'm just trying to release this weight that's
pulling me down
If I say I just need to cry
I just need to get it out
I promise I'm not giving you the run around

Do Not Disturb

My phone's on D N D
I'm busy
Recharging
I need a moment to just breathe
Another to just be

Longing

Longing for connection
To be seen
And deeply known
To be free
Rather it can be freeing
I miss being surrounded by my family
Visiting
Hanging out
Connecting
I miss the light atmosphere
With laughter and joy filling the space all around
us
I miss the wisdom of my grandmother
She always knows what to say
No matter the situation
Maybe that's where my dad gets it from
His empathy and compassion
My dad.
I miss my dad
I love him dearly

Outlier

You ever feel like an outlier to the family you
were born into?
I mean Yea all ya uncles and aunties
Cousins and grannies
Extended family
They love you
They know about you
Maybe even care to some degree
Yet there's still some sort of disconnect
Like we're all in the cafeteria
Eating at different tables
And no one wants to sit with me
I mean they stop by
They visit
But no one eats with me
Not the family I was given anyways
There's not many at my table
And I'm grateful for the ones who eat with me
I just can't help anticipate and wonder
When will their seat become empty
Then I'll truly be all alone
Like I am now
Sitting here writing this
Alone
I mean I guess it doesn't have to be a bad thing

I just long for connection
Real
Genuine
Connection
Where I am enough
And I don't have to pretend to be someone I'm
not
I don't have to bend and twist to fit in a mold
Where I can just be
As I was created to be
A human being

To be an Adult

Learning what it means to be an adult

To be an adult is to do things even when you
don't want to
And this shit sucks
It's being disciplined
Making decisions
Even the ones you don't want
Because they aren't pleasing
It's showing up as you are and giving what you
can
Whether it's 5%
2 or even 10
It's knowing yea I want a burger for dinner from
this one place but it'll leave me constipated
So instead buying groceries to have a hearty
home cooked meal
It's I want to play video games or watch Netflix
today and the house needs to be cleaned and
having to do that first
Even if it means no Netflix or video games
It's I feel like shit, hate my job, and wanna quit
Teasing the idea of calling out or being late
And knowing that I have bills to pay so I can't
afford to not have a job.

Having a stinky attitude
Because becoming an adult is a load of shit
I was never really one to play with dolls
I played with words over paper and pen
Toying with thoughts about life
What I want
What I hoped it to be
Adulthood didn't quite live up to what I thought
it'd be
And that's okay
Because there are moments
Where it's exactly what I need it to be
Where I can relish in the comfort of my own
space
With the person I love
Where I can be free to be me
And not have to live up to anybody's
expectations
Where it's just me and this version of me who
I've yet to meet
Adulthood isn't everything I hoped it to be
But it's growing on me

Honest

If we're being honest
I'm afraid to be alone
Afraid of myself
So I focus on everyone else
And when everyone leaves
I find other ways to distract
Now I'm out of places to hide
And no where to run
It's just me myself and her
That little girl who took on so much alone
Who always had to be strong even when it was
too much
I wish I could see what everyone else sees
"Sweet, loving, kind, pretty, beautiful"
Instead all I hear are demons and insecurities
screaming lies at me
"You're too much "
"No one has time for you"
"What you want doesn't matter"
"You're needs aren't important"
So I sat quiet and alone
Searching for someone or something to prove
them wrong
You came along
Proved them wrong

But somehow some way they found a loop hole
and I'm still not enough
Man I wish I could break out of this stupid little
ball
Running out air
Running out of time
Is this the way I die?
Sad and alone?
To that little girl I'm so sorry I left you all alone
I'm sorry I abandoned myself
To try and find what I needed in them
When we had it all along
I'm sorry I kept straying away from home
Old habits ,die hard I suppose
I'm sorry I was and am so afraid of you
Of me
Of myself
I'm turning over a new leaf I suppose
Diving head first into the things that scare me
Maybe there's nothing to be scared of after all